Keep Them Thinking

· Level I ·

A Handbook of Model Lessons

Kay Opeka

Skylight Publishing, Inc.
Palatine, Illinois

Other Books in This Series:

Catch Them Thinking

Teach Them Thinking

Start Them Thinking

Keep Them Thinking: Level II

Keep Them Thinking: Level III

Keep Them Thinking: Level I
Second Edition, Second Printing

Published by Skylight Publishing, 200 E. Wood Street, Suite 274, Palatine, Illinois 60067

Editing: Robin Fogarty and Sharon Nowakowski
Type Composition and Formatting: Donna Ramirez
Book Design: Bruce Leckie
Production Coordination: Ari Ohlson

Printed in the United States of America

Library of Congress Catalog Card Number 91-61813

ISBN 0-932935-34-6

Foreword

Our children are the messages we send to a time we will not see.
—Betty Seigle

The lessons in this series are designed with three premises in mind: The teacher is the architect of the intellect, the student is the capable apprentice and thinking is more basic than the basics—it frames all learning.

Premise 1 — The Teacher Is The Architect Of The Intellect

A teacher affects eternity. He never knows where his influence ends.

—Henry Adams

As an architect of the intellect, a teacher leaves his mark on history. The classroom teacher is, above all else, a designer of learning, an expert craftsman who knows content, understands child development, and manages young people with finesse.

The excellent teacher skillfully crafts the lesson with a clear purpose. Just as form follows function for the traditional architect, the structure of the lesson is determined by the learning goal.

Aesthetically, lessons are designed to invite the learner in. When the design is exquisite, the invitation becomes irresistible to the learner. He enters the learning situation excited and with a level of expectancy that sets the scene for motivated learning.

Premise 2 — The Student Is The Capable Apprentice

Come to the edge, he said. They said: We are afraid.
Come to the edge, he said. They came.
He pushed them...and they flew.

—Apollinaire

Believing that the student is capable of becoming the master of his own learning is sometimes difficult for the architect mentor. But through carefully crafted instruction, exemplary, consistent modeling and deliberate practice, the apprentice learns. Only then, by relinquishing the honored role of master architect, is the student free to advance on his own.

To believe one is capable is to let go. It is to trust and to watch as the learner takes over—and goes beyond—for he is the capable apprentice.

Premise 3   Thinking Is More Basic Than The Basics

Intelligent behavior is knowing what to do when you don't know what to do.

—*Arthur Costa*

Thinking is the foundation for all learning. To say we're going to teach thinking in our classroom does not imply that we don't already do just that. Of course we teach thinking, but now by focusing on cognitive behavior, thinking becomes the blueprint by which we design and structure learning.

The blueprint of thinking becomes the reference that guides our instructional decisions. And, as the architect of the intellect, we concern ourselves as much with the process as with the final product. We select materials with care and deliberation. We direct activities with skill and closely monitor the progress. Finally, with a feeling of pride and accomplishment, we stand back and view the masterpiece—in this case a cadre of young people—thinking and learning in self-directed ways.

Robin Fogarty
Editor

Contents

Introduction vii

Creative Thinking Skill: Idea Collecting—Informal Brainstorming 1
Explicit Skill Model Lesson 2
Short Practices 9
Transfer Lesson in Creative Writing 10
Transfer Lesson in Health/Body Skeleton 11
Transfer Lesson in Language Arts/Printed Materials
   and Periodicals 12
Evaluation of Skills 13

Critical Thinking Skill: Identifying Attributes 15
Explicit Skill Model Lesson 16
Short Practices 19
Transfer Lesson in Kinesthetics/Math and Art 20
Transfer Lesson in Literature/Language Arts 22
Transfer Lesson in Natural Sciences/Rock Awareness 26
Evaluation of Skills 28

Problem-Solving Skill: Finding Problems and Solutions 29
Explicit Skill Model Lesson 30
Short Practices 34
Transfer Lesson in Literature 37
Transfer Lesson in Art/Situational Problems 39
Evaluation of Skills 41

Masters Appendix   43
Premise 1
Premise 2
Premise 3
Idea Collecting (Brainstorming) Guidelines
Today's Brain Game
Evaluation of Skills
Attribute Grid
Rock Classifications
Evaluation of Skills

Osborn's 3 Steps To Problem Solving
Sample Problem-Solving Activity
Idea Map
Evaluation of Skills

Worksheet Model for Original Lessons   57

Bibliography   61

Introduction

With the understanding that students begin to develop their thinking skills at a very early age, *Keep Them Thinking: Level I* presents lessons and activities designed especially for grades K-4. These lessons cover three different areas of thinking—creative, critical, and problem solving—and detail a spectrum of mental processes ready to be practiced and taught in the elementary classroom.

Creative Thinking

The first section introduces students to informal brainstorming processes through the creative thinking skill of **idea collecting**. The transfer lessons included in this section demonstrate ways to use idea collecting processes in promoting multiple ideas, increasing student motivation and applying reinforcement to any content area lesson or skill. This creative processing causes students to generate and produce many ideas as they associate and piggyback on each other's thinking.

Critical Thinking

In the second section, students practice **identifying attributes** to foster their critical thinking abilities. The detailed transfer lessons demonstrate that all students can learn and practice critical thinking as it is transferred into lessons in math, science and literature. This skill requires students to analyze and evaluate information as they process data.

Problem Solving

Both creative, generative processes and critical, analytical processes are promoted in the third section to help students in **finding problems and solutions**. The basic problem-solving model that is introduced focuses on the problem-finding, idea-finding and solution-finding processes of the Parnes and Noller Creative Problem-Solving Model. The lessons included in this chapter allow students to process familiar situations encountered both at home or at school.

Explicit Lessons

For each thinking skill you will find an explicit teaching model with highlighted information and notes. This elaborated model provides a prototype or template for you to adopt in designing other explicit thinking skill lessons, practice exercises and transfer activities.

The **MODEL LESSONS** include:

Lesson Objective The new skill for the lesson explicitly stated.

Key Vocabulary Vocabulary that may require clarification, explanation and/or emphasis before, during and after the lesson.

Looking Back A brief statement to stir prior knowledge to help relate the new information to previous experiences.

Getting Ready Background information, rationale and premises that undergird the lesson.

At-A-Glance A synopsis of the lesson or the lesson in a nutshell.

Materials A quick reference list of all the materials you will need for the model lesson.

Focus Activity A short, anticipatory activity suggested to set the stage for the introduction of the new skill.

Activity Objective A concise statement of the purpose of the main activity.

Activity The interactive part of the classroom lesson, including the instructional input and the student participation.

Metacognitive Processing Reflective questions, activities and discussion ideas about the lesson and the new skill.

Practice

To ensure internalization of the skills, short practices are outlined after the model lesson. The **Short Practices** offer suggestions for using the skills in your lessons and provide examples of exercises for relating that skill to familiar situations in students' everyday lives.

Transfer

Specifically tailored to activities in a variety of subject areas, the **Transfer Lessons** delineate the ease of bridging thinking skills across the curriculum. These shortened versions of the model lessons include: **Focus Activity, Objective, Activity, Metacognitive Processing** and **Follow-up** (lesson extensions and enrichment ideas for both in and out of the classroom).

Evaluation

As a final step in ensuring student transfer and understanding of the thinking skills presented, each chapter concludes with an **Evaluation of Skills**. You may use this section to further process the activities with your students or to measure, gauge or evaluate your students' development and comprehension of the lessons.

Ongoing Transfer

View the lessons as generic patterns upon which to model personally relevant lesson plans for the teaching of critical and creative thinking. Enjoy the activities and their flexibility in teaching students cognitive skills as thinking becomes an integral part of all that we do in our interactions with students.

Creative Thinking
Level I

Idea Collecting

Thinking Skill:

Idea Collecting

Children are not vessels to be filled but lamps to be lighted.
—Author Unknown

Model Lesson:

Lesson Objective To introduce the technique of informal brainstorming, idea collecting.

Key Vocabulary Idea collecting, piggybacking, brain games.

Looking Back From previous experiences, students will have had opportunities to orally share ideas in group situations and in focused discussions.

Getting Ready You need not worry that brainstorming will add another "burden" to an already heavy schedule because it "plants so many seeds" among the children, enriches activities and raises learning levels. In fact, the process creates products usable in both skill instruction and curriculum enrichment.

As you work with young students you are, or will quickly become, aware of their short attention spans, natural self-centeredness, contagious exuberance and simple honesty—all of which enhance class brainstorming activities.

Because young students have such short attention spans, they need to begin informal brainstorming activities directed toward the familiar. If the subject is not appropriate or the time period is too extended, students will find a new activity in which to partake—either alone or with a neighbor—and you will have lost the opportunity to begin the development of brainstorming skills.

As a young student's world is just beginning to expand, he/she is naturally self-centered. For students, waiting to share ideas is very difficult, and at times, impossible. But, what young students lack in attention spans and group dynamics, they make up in enthusiastic, contagious participation in new experiences.

The simple honesty of young students provides fertile ground for brainstorming. Their ideas often reveal new and refreshing looks at the regular or ordinary. Build on this natural trait, being careful so as not to stifle their ideas and enthusiasm.

Brainstorming techniques, when learned and practiced in the classroom, enable teachers to involve all students in a group learning activity. The values derived from encouraging and permitting your students to begin sharing opinions and ideas early in their education will strengthen their basic skill development and enrich curriculum activities.

At-A-Glance Initiate the idea of collecting concrete items and abstract words by discussing personal collections. Next, introduce the Brain Game rules and procedures. Model the brainstorming, idea collecting, activity from inception to utilization involving various participants. Discuss the procedures and follow up with transfer activities across various curriculum areas.

Materials Needed

- ☐ Idea Collecting (Brainstorming) Guidelines (handouts or transparency)

- ☐ Lined chart paper

- ☐ Masking tape

- ☐ Marking pencils

- ☐ Timer

- ☐ Sample Brain Game transparency

- ☐ Access to copier for duplication of lists

Focus Activity Ask the students: Who has a collection at home? Tell me about your collection. Why did you start collecting_____? Where do you find_____? What are some things other people and students might collect? Practice using *wait time,* a three- to ten-second pause after a question, to allow students time to think.

Activity Objective To ensure fluency, understanding and procedure development with a subject in which the students have a high level of knowledge.

Activity

1. Choose a high-attention time period for the students (we cannot expect them to be fluent and creative when they are tired or hungry) and bring them together on the story rug or the regular group area.

2. Have the marking pencils readily available and the chart paper positioned so all students can see it.

3. Introduce brainstorming as "idea collecting"—young students understand collecting and collections. Explain that you are going to help them make a collection of their ideas by writing what they share. Do not use the word *brainstorming*. It is too literal for young students, and your planned objective will be lost in its explanation.

4. Announce to the students: "We are going to learn a brain game. You have to be good listeners and use your brain. The game will start when I set this timer. The game ends when the bell on this timer rings. Listen...." If students are unfamiliar with what and how a timer works, spend a few minutes explaining and sharing.

5. Next, practice collecting ideas on a topic familiar to your students— cartoon characters, letters, farm animals, colors, types of breakfast food etc.—using the Brain Game.

Idea Collecting (Brainstorming) Guidelines

- Record ideas exactly as stated, (including duplicates).
- Withhold all comments.
- Remind (by example, not by a statement) students to piggyback on other ideas.
- Eliminate the time limit if students are experienced enough at idea collecting.
- Review the list visually and orally.
- Remove duplicates.
- Guess how many ideas were collected.
- Count the actual number of ideas.
- Recount them in another way.
- Compare the guesses with the actual count.
- Use the originals and duplicates again and again.

The Brain Game

1. Recording The Ideas

a. Tell them it's time to start the game and set the timer. With younger students, start with a two- or three-minute time limit.

b. Print one of your topic "ideas" on the chart paper to get the students started.

c. Print quickly and carefully, repeating each student's idea as you record it.

d. Accept all ideas without praise or comment.

e. Record duplicates when named.

f. If a lull occurs, that's OK. Be patient and let the students think. . . .

g. If an extended lull occurs, you may want to show students how to piggyback (associate) off of others' ideas to encourage student thinking.

h. When the timer rings, stop the activity.

2. Reviewing The Ideas

a. Reread each idea or let the students read them if possible. As you go through the list, use your hand to highlight the word or words being read.

b. Students will usually call your attention to duplicated ideas during the review. If they do not comment, you might suggest there is a problem in your collection of ideas or words; can they tell you what it is? Make every attempt not to "point it out." They will either discover it visually, orally or by realizing someone repeated "their idea."
Important: Remove the second idea. Students remember who "said it first."

3. Counting The Ideas

a. After reviewing the items and eliminating duplicates, extend the activity to include an oral, group counting experience. As with most collections, students will want to count the number of ideas they shared. This will encourage fluency the next time you collect ideas.

b. Comment favorably on students' abilities to share ideas. Refer to the group discussion about collecting and collections, repeating a particular students's collection. For example: "John has 18 Hot Wheels in his collection. I wonder how many_____we have on our list. (Cover or fold the list of words.) Before we count, let's *guess* how many ideas we collected today."

c. Record on the chalkboard the estimates from students who want to take a guess. Be aware of the noncontributor. You might ask that child, "Mary, will you share your guess? This is not a right or wrong game. This is a guessing game."

d. When the guesses (without the contributors' names) are posted, reveal the list of collected ideas and tell the students, "Let's count the ideas together." Using your hand, move down the list slowly, specifically zeroing in on oral counting.

e. On the list, record and circle the total number with a large, colorful numeral. Say: "We started at the very top, now we need to recount to be sure we counted correctly. Can anyone suggest where we might start counting this time?"

f. Recount from the bottom!

g. Compare the actual count with students' guesses by asking relevant questions such as: "Can someone find the exact same number on both lists? Which number is closest to the actual count?"

h. "When we play guessing games, everybody should take a guess. Sometimes we are right . . . sometimes we are wrong. That's OK as long as we try."

4. Using The Ideas/Words

a. After you have incorporated brainstorming skills and activities into your teaching, use the lists—and photocopies of the lists—from your Brain Game activities in transfer ring the skill into different areas of the curriculum. Each list of collected ideas provides an extensive amount of words and topics for language experiences, instructional writing and creative writing. Use these topics and words!

b. Uses for original list:

At a later date post the original list of ideas so all students can see it. The ideas should be printed neatly and large enough for instructional purposes.

Discuss the collection of ideas and demonstrate how we can piggyback new ones. Using one of the recorded ideas, give an example of how one idea may spur others. For example, If brainstorming zoo animals, the suggestion *monkey* might stimulate thoughts of apes or gorillas.

Sample Lesson

1. Read the original list *to* or *with* the class (depending on their abilities).

2. Tell the students that they all will have an opportunity to choose one animal to dictate a sentence about and they will be able to take that sentence home to share.

3. Demonstrate the activity: "I'm going to choose the giraffe. My sentence is, 'The giraffe has a long, skinny neck.'"

4. Record it on a strip of paper; use "said" phrases and proper punctuation.

> Mrs. Opeka said, "The giraffe has a long, skinny neck."

5. Ask, "Who would like to choose an animal and dictate a sentence to me about that animal?"

6. After recording and rereading the sentence, encourage the student to take

it home to share. Communications to parents might suggest that when their child brings home an animal sentence, he/she can draw a picture of it, find a picture of it or choose a library book about that animal.

7. This activity should be done in short segments of 5 to 10 minutes, recording two or three sentences at a time. If you extend the period, students' enthusiasm will diminish. Return to the activity when you have another 10 minutes. Be sure to schedule the time in your daily plans—all students must have the opportunity to dictate a sentence to bring home.

c. Uses for duplicated lists:

Pass out copies of the original lists of students' collected ideas. The ideas should be printed neatly and large enough for instructional purposes.

Have students find common letters, words, vowels or consonants among the ideas on their lists by finger pointing, circling, underlining or highlighting with yellow or orange crayons. For example, have them find the word *zebra*, the letter *D*, two words that begin with *B* or something else appropriate for their ability level.

Note: Yellow crayons may be best for highlighting because they are visual, they do not demand fine motor control, and their "leads" do not break.

Metacognitive Processing

1. To encourage student participation in *divergent* thinking, communications with parents must be ongoing and meaningful. Therefore, the students' collection of ideas should be printed, duplicated and sent home as soon as possible. Parents who are involved with their children's education will often pick up on the activity and encourage additional ideas.

In a classroom where useful material and information go home regularly, a copy of Today's Brain Game will be appreciated and helpful. Have the students tell their parents *how* they made the list. Review the sample brain game on the next page.

TODAY'S BRAIN GAME
ROOM 101

September 9

ball	book	boot
bat	bee	barn
boat	buzz	bird
balloon	bumble bee	buzzard
box	banana	butterfly
Bob	BIG	bake
Bobby	bed	bacon

Today we collected _____ *words starting with the letter b* _____ in class.

You may wish to spend a few minutes reviewing and extending the "idea collecting" (brainstorming) activity by letting or helping your child do one or more of the following:
  • Discover more *b* items in your house, magazines and conversations.
  • Color all the *b*'s on the list yellow or orange.
  • Count the *k*'s on the list or on a page in a magazine.
  • Find the letters that are in his/her own name.
  • Find the longest word on the list.

Enjoy! Enjoy! Remember, 10 to 15 minutes is adequate and valuable! Thanks for your help.

Sample Brain Game

2. You also can encourage student participation in divergent thinking activities by having students share their lists of collected ideas and by having them invite other students to add new ideas.

For example, to prepare for a creative writing list your class may want to collect winter words. You can:

• Publish a list in the school newspaper or bulletin requesting additional ideas be sent to your classroom.

- Display your list outside the classroom with an appropriate eye-catcher such as "We Named 72 Winter Words! We would like to reach 100. Can you help us?"

- Send a written challenge to another classroom for a "Winter Word List" competition. Plan the activity for the same day, in the same time limits and with similar preparations.

Short Practices:

Use of the creative thinking skill divergent thinking provides you with a list of words or phrases that are meaningful to the students and from which you can teach other skills. These lists of collected ideas can become valuable teaching tools—think *daily brainstorming* for one of the following applications.

FOR ALL STUDENTS

■ To increase student motivation, introduce a new unit, a new skill or a new book by collecting ideas. This will set the focus and give you information about how much the students already know.

■ To apply reinforcement to a lesson, practice a skill in a group activity so that student input is necessary and idea collecting is practiced. For example, if you are studying nouns, collect a list of nouns.

■ To provide an effective wrap-up for a unit or lesson, have students collect a list of ideas for a creative writing project.

■ To promote problem solving, gather student input on organization, socialization or management problems in the classroom using the brainstorming techniques structured in this chapter.

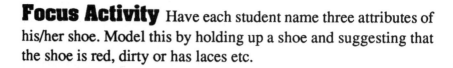

Transfer Lesson:
Creative Writing

Focus Activity Have each student name three attributes of his/her shoe. Model this by holding up a shoe and suggesting that the shoe is red, dirty or has laces etc.

Objective To provide multiple ideas for each of four elements that might be found in a group story or individual stories.

Activity

1. Choose a curriculum area from which you want to do a creative writing activity and identify four elements for story development. For example, for the topic *circus* you might choose to develop circus people, circus animals, circus purchases or food, and who goes to the circus.

2. Make a large, four-column grid. On day one tell students that today's brain game will provide us with a list of circus people.

3. Record the ideas by following the informal brainstorming guidelines in the Brain Game.

4. Review the list of ideas collected by the students.

5. On day two, collect a list of animals in the circus and review the list.

6. On day three, collect a list of things you can buy or eat at the circus.

7. On day four, collect a list of people who go to the circus.

8. For a creative writing project, whether for group or individual stories, choose one item from each column to create a story with pictures and/or a circus mural.

9. The choice from each column should be objective, not subjective—for example, draw a number "out of a hat," have students give you four numbers (previous to explaining the purpose of the four numbers), use the year, use the date etc. Be original in establishing which four elements will be story criteria.

Metacognitive Processing
Word lists created by students for creative writing motivate, stimulate and generally enrich the writing process and the final product. Use them frequently! Talk about how the list grows—how to piggyback—by associating and by generating new ideas from old ideas.

Follow-up Have ongoing word lists displayed in the classroom. Encourage students to add, share and use new words. For example, find words for *said*, *good* and *big*. If students participate in brainstorming these lists, you increase the possibility of students using them and the brainstorming techniques.

Transfer Lesson:
Health/ Body Skeleton

Focus Activity Displaying a wishbone and a dog bone, have students collect ideas of other types of bones.

Objective To provide high-interest motivation for a health unit on the body skeleton through divergent thinking.

Activity

1. Present the word *ancon*.

2. Ask students to share their ideas by predicting:
   a. "What do you think it means?"
   b. "What do you think it is?"

3. Record all ideas by following the informal brainstorming guidelines in the Brain Game.

4. Do not give the answer. Suggest that they find out what it means on their own time!

5. The next day, begin the skeleton unit. (Ancon is another name for elbow.)

Metacognitive Processing Discuss the meaning of the word *ancon*. How/where did students find answers to what *ancon* might be or mean?

Ask students to share the thoughts and connections they had while collecting ideas about the new word. Ask, "What made you think an ancon was *a big snake,* or *a little nut*?" Permit discussion to track the associative thinking that took place with the students.

Follow-up Introduce the Thinking Log as a place for students to catch, track, note or elaborate upon any of their ideas. Have the students draw their version of an ancon in their Thinking Logs.

Transfer Lesson:

Language Arts/ Printed Materials and Periodicals

Focus Activity Displaying a T.V. Guide or Sears Catalog, have students collect ideas of what they might find inside the pages.

Objective To introduce components of a newspaper to the students and to discover how to use the components as teaching tools.

Activity

1. Begin the activity: "This is a daily newspaper. What do you know or think you can find inside the pages?"

2. Record all of the students' ideas by following the informal brainstorming guidelines in the Brain Game.

3. You might add an idea or two relevant to the ability level of your students to get them started on the activity.

4. Review the final list as a group.

5. Break into small groups of no more than three persons for the next step in this activity.

6. Give each group a newspaper and one (or more) of the collected items to locate.

7. Depending on your class' ability level, have students locate the items and
   a. circle or highlight
   b. cut out
   c. identify by page number

8. Share the ideas from this activity in a large group circle. Did the groups find many items or few?

9. Items not located by a small group should be discussed. Are they or aren't they in a newspaper? Why or why not?

10. Any new newspaper components discovered by the small groups can be added to the original collection of ideas.

Metacognitive Processing Cut up and re-sequence a comic strip that is age appropriate. Talk about how to decide on the order and other possibilities for ordering it.

Follow-up Begin an ongoing bulletin board with newspaper parts labeled for identification.

Write a daily headline (in all capitals and with a minimum number of words) about a class activity, a school activity or a "special student."

Evaluation of Skills:

After completing initial lessons in brainstorming techniques say: "When we ride the school bus we have to follow some rules. When we collect ideas (brainstorm) we also have rules."

Depending on your students' ages, levels and abilities, do one of the following evaluative processes—not for content, but for understanding of the SKILL OF IDEA COLLECTING.

1. Have the students dictate ideas/rules about collecting ideas for a Language Experience Chart to be displayed in the room.

2. Have the students draw pictures of a class idea collecting. Ask the students to dictate or write sentences about the activity.

3. Have the students record in their Thinking Logs:

    Three things I know about idea collecting are

    (1)_____

    (2)_____

    (3)_____

Critical Thinking
Level I

Identifying Attributes

Thinking Skill:

Identifying Attributes

To classify is to bring order into existence:. . .it encourages children to make order out of their own world, to think on their own, to come to their own conclusions.

—Louis E. Raths

Model Lesson:

Lesson Objective To help students identify differences and likenesses, classify and form groups using one or more critical attributes.

Key Vocabulary Alike, different, group, sets, attributes, subsets, critical attributes

Looking Back Students will have some understanding of differences and likenesses. They will be knowledgeable about forming groups and sets of things from sorting activities done at home or at school.

Getting Ready In preparation for attribute identification, we are aware that even toddlers begin to group items without verbalizing "this attribute" or "that attribute." When playing with a mixed set of blocks or a conglomeration of plastic animals, young children will group the items using attribute identifications logical for their developmental age. When we begin to move students into abstract learning, we should not ignore the skills in manipulative grouping and the process of identifying critical attributes.

A group of anything has like qualities. . .it may also have differences. We need to expect student identification of these like attributes and to encourage new possibilities for multiple groupings (subsets).

Attributes are identified through one's senses. Being aware that we can see, hear, feel, taste and even smell attributes justifies the need for students to be aware of groupings that occur every day in their lives. Because much will depend on this mental ability to group, we need to practice and apply the *process* of attribute identification.

At-A-Glance Initiate attribute identification by stimulating interest in naming attributes (use the word *attributes*) of a familiar item. Next, model a lesson in attribute identification using participants. Discuss the process, follow up with practice, do a transfer lesson and evaluate.

Focus Activity Hold up an item (a familiar item) for everyone in the class to see. Ask the students how they would describe this item to someone unfamiliar with it. List on the chart paper the students' attributes and descriptions.

Activity Objective To determine deductively (i.e. using a label and fitting the students *to* the label) what groupings can be made from identifiable attributes and to determine inductively what critical attributes are identifiable in groupings (i.e. placing students together and developing a generalization or label.)

Materials Needed

☐ Familiar item (watch, potato, pencil, apple)

☐ Chart paper

☐ Chart stand or masking tape

☐ Marking pencils

Activity

1. Choose 5 to 15 minutes that have been planned and written into your daily plans and bring the students together in a group.

2. Tell them, "We are going to play a brain game." Remind them that they will need to think, watch and listen. Ask someone to guess how many students are in the group. Let other students guess. Give your guess, then count the number of students out loud. This reinforces estimation by guessing and gives students a relevant short practice.

3. Say, "We have a group of 23 children. They are all third graders. What else can you tell me? For example: They all live in_____. They all go to _____ school. They all are in room _____. I'm going to make some new groups. I will want to know why the students were put in these new groups."

4. Form a group of students wearing tennis shoes, blue slacks, hair clips, buckle shoes or any critical attribute you determine is appropriate for the age level and population of your class. Have one student move at a time, slowly add more students to the new group.

5. If someone guesses what the critical attribute is before all students are grouped, encourage that student to finish the grouping. When the activity is completed, ask the student to explain how the critical attribute was found. Help with clarifying questions. Remember, if the student discovered the critical attribute, the student had a method. It is important to listen and to be patient. Allow the student time to think it through and to discover the strategy. Give positive feedback about the child's personal way of thinking.

6. If no one guesses the critical attribute, use a technique to help in discovering the attribute: Form two lines facing each other and let them observe. If more help is needed, work from head down (or toes up) asking questions such as, "Do you see anything the same or different about the others' hair . . . eyes . . . ears?"

7. Once the critical attribute is identified, discuss which senses helped in the process of discovering it and talk through the process.

8. If a group's critical attribute was buckles on the student's shoes, remember to identify a second group, that which has no buckles! With these groupings, you are laying excellent groundwork for comparing with Venn diagrams.

9. Reorganize students into one large group. Ask if someone wants to make a new grouping. Trust a child's grouping process. If "it" doesn't work, the student will discover the problem. Help the student out of the situation if necessary, but don't change the attribute. You may have to clarify, broaden or narrow the original choice. Wait patiently, call on a variety of children and give "Hurrahs!"

10. Encourage a new grouping as time and capabilities permit. **Remember:** Have students verbalize what attribute identifies the new group. Ask how they happened to choose that particular attribute. When students become more skilled, add another attribute—for example, a girl *with* a barrette.

Metacognitive Processing

1. Lead students in a discussion about how they look for attributes, how they use their senses to detect likenesses and differences, and how looking for patterns helps us group things.

2. Have students respond in turn with the first thing that pops into their heads for this sentence. "Sometimes I put things in groups when I _____."

3. End with a group hurrah!

Short Practices:

Students need numerous opportunities to recognize critical attributes. When they have grouped *themselves* many times, practice with other items and words.

FOR YOUNGER STUDENTS

■ Gather about five students together during free time or small-group time. Dump a "mixed mess" of blocks, tinker-toys, plastic snappers or something similar. Ask the students how they can make some new groups or subsets. Let them go! As you have the opportunity to observe, ask why and what else might work? You can stimulate fluency by suggesting a group, just don't over do it!

FOR OLDER STUDENTS

■ Either prepare "junk bags" from drawers, desks and closets or have students put 15 to 20 things in a bag from their desks, pockets or wherever. Have the students work in pairs to create subsets, new groups. Allow (in fact, encourage) talking and explaining of attributes that are identifiable. You can offer and encourage extensions to their ideas by reminding them to use their senses. They should also show their work by recording the varied attributes they identify and to which set/sets an item might belong. They can begin to establish "rules" for their groupings as they reason inductively from the specifics to a generalization.

Students can make subsets and have another group reason deductively (from the general to the specific) to determine other things that will "fit" the grouping.

FOR ALL STUDENTS

■ Place individual name cards (about 3" x 8") in a pocket chart. Use a name list with older students. Discuss that the group has many names (give the exact number) and that numerous sub-groups can be made by using the visual clues of the letters and words in those names. Make one sample subset of the names that is appropriate to your class' developmental level—for example, it starts with the letter *b*, there are two vowels, it has one syllable etc. Give students time to work on finding different subsets. Extend the activity over a few days. If a student identifies only one name as a group and no others fit the criteria . . . that's OK! The identification of an attribute is the skill, not the number of items in a group.

■ Use the lists your class created to practice divergent, creative thinking. The items and words can be grouped by visual clues, language or definitions. **Important:** Encourage thinking time, sharing time and tell-me-why time. The more opportunities students have to practice attribute identification, the better they will understand and master the skill. Lots of short practices interspersed throughout the day will help students begin to use attributing as a pattern for thinking—a way to organize their thinking.

Transfer Lesson:

Kinesthetics/ Math and Art

Focus Activity Have students brainstorm words about clay as you give them chunks of clay. (Save a piece for yourself for demonstrating later.)

Objective To infuse attribute identification practice into the math and art curricula while encouraging small motor activity and vocabulary development.

Activity

1. Tell students to soften their clay (by squeezing, rolling, kneading it etc.) while you share some new words with them. Say, repeat and write on the board the words *sphere, cylinder, cube* and *cone*. Use the phrases *rectangular solid, circle solid* etc. if age-appropriate.

2. Ask all students to roll their clay into a sphere. Demonstrate. When they look at yours and say, "That's a ball," tell them a sphere is like a ball and today we will learn its other name, sphere.

3. Say, "Tell me something about your sphere." Accept comparisons to a ball or the sun, but work toward a common iden-

tifying attributes, such as it has no flat sides, it rolls, it goes round and round, it's smooth etc.

4. Using the word *sphere*, brainstorm a list of things shaped like a sphere.

5. "Let's add an attribute to our spheres today. " For example, "Let's poke two pencil holes in our clay spheres. Our spheres have two pencil holes. Do all spheres have to have holes? Why or why not?"

6. "Now put your clay sphere on the table and roll it into a cylinder —not a skinny one—make it a fat cylinder. Now tap each end gently. (Demonstrate.) What can you tell me about a cylinder? What do you see? Look at the ends. What are some attributes of a cylinder?"

7. Collect a list of cylinder-shaped items.

8. Have students make a sphere again. Say: "Show me your spheres. OK, now we're going to make a cube. That's just like a box, dice or a counting block. (Show items if students need visual clues.) If you tap the sides of your sphere gently you can make a cube." Demonstrate.

9. "Look carefully at your cube. What do you see? Let's count the sides. Can you name some attributes of a cube?"

10. "Do you see any cubes in our room?" Allow ample time for recognition, identification and justifications.

Metacognitive Processing
Have students choose one shape to make. You may want to let them practice three or four shapes first. As you move around the room, ask the students: "Which shape do you make best? Why? Which shape was the most difficult to create? Why?" Have students group themselves by the shapes they made. Count how many there are of each kind. Name at least one attribute of a chosen shape and discuss why more spheres (if that's the case) and less cubes were made.

In an activity like this, many students will identify their shapes by what they are not—that's OK. If it's not flat, not a cylinder and not egg-shaped, but it rolls, it just might be a sphere!

Follow-up
Allow students free time with clay. Some students will create more shapes and will discuss attributes of their creations

even though they may be unaware they are doing the process. Others may just want to create original, nondescriptive sculptures.

Transfer Lesson:
Literature/ Language Arts

Focus Activity Have students compare the similarities and differences between two books.

Objective To identify attributes of both fiction and nonfiction books.

Activity

1. Add a collection of 12 animal books to your classroom library by choosing six animals and selecting a fiction and nonfiction book about each one. For example:

   Timothy Turtle, by Al Graham
   The Turtle Book, by Mel Crawford

   The Story of Babar, by Jean DeBrunhoff
   Elephants, by Isobel Beard

   Danny and the Dinosaur, by Syd Hoff
   Giant Dinosaurs, by Erna Rowe

   These are only examples. Consider using monkeys, dogs, cats, mice, rabbits, pandas and even koalas.

Attribute Grid

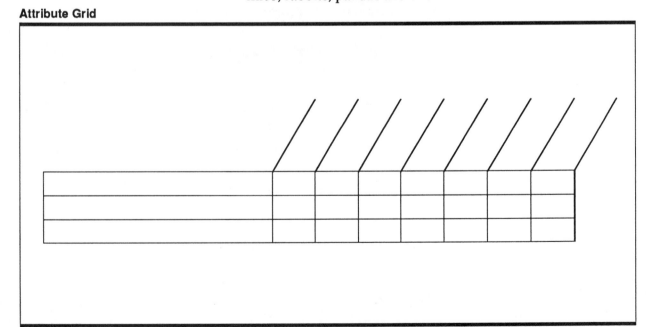

2. Have a large grid on a bulletin board or transparency prepared for listing the names of the 12 books you will be using. (See the attribute grid below.)

3. Place the collection of animal books and 10 to 15 additional books in the middle of a circle of students. Ask what kind of a group or set it is. When identified as books, ask what attribute makes them books. With follow-up questions, arrive at the critical attribute of printed material in a bound form. A printed newspaper is not a book. Older students should explore additional attributes of why a book is a book.

4. Say: "Let's make some new groups or subsets. Who has an idea?" As students suggest size, color, animals etc., have the books moved physically to their new group. Ask students to identify the critical attribute of each new group.

5. Be aware of the opportunity (if students are ready) to expose them to Venn diagrams without formal introduction. You can encircle a group of red books and a group of large books with chalk or yarn. The students may find difficulty in placing a large, red book. Use wait time, think time. Do not jump in with the solution too quickly. Go with the opportunity. (See the Venn diagram below.)

Venn Diagram

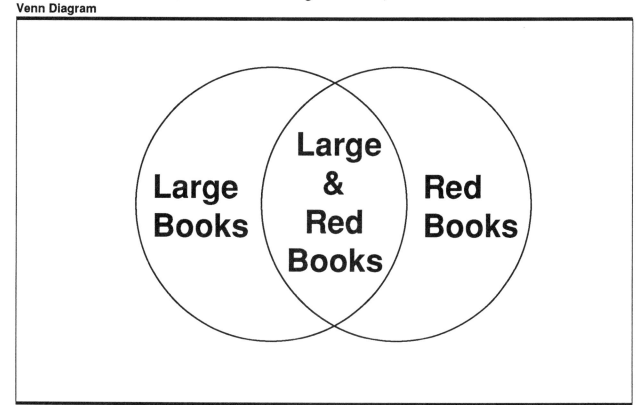

Categories must be age or
ability appropriate

Book	Hard Cover	Soft Cover	Title Page	Table of Contents	Pictures	Animals Talking	Animals Not Talking

Book Attribute Grid

6. Read an age-appropriate, *nonfiction* animal book in class. Identify book elements such as cover, title, title page, table of contents, pictures and index. Explain that this is called a nonfiction book or an information book. Ask: "Why is that a good name? What information did you learn? Did the book tell you something real or make-believe? Give me some examples." Use the large grid on the bulletin board to list all the attributes identified. (See the book attribute grid above and the FOLLOW-UP section on the next page for examples and suggestions.)

7. Now show a *fiction* book about the same animal. Identify the elements of a book, noting any physical similarities or differences it has with the nonfiction book. Next, read the book in class.

8. Discuss the book's content: "Is this real or make-believe? How do you know? What is one clue? Can you think of another clue? Let's look at the two books together." When choosing nonfiction books for your class, look for ones with actual photographs that will look distinctly different from the pictures in the fiction books.

9. Each day read two books about one animal. The extensions are limitless depending on your writing and science curricula. Teachers read to students every day. Why not include critical thinking in the process?

Metacognitive Processing For younger students, include a parent involvement activity with the next homebound library book. For example, send home an activity similar to the following:

We have been working on special kinds of attributes (characteristics of books). I need to tell you three attributes about the book _____:

(1)_____

(2)_____

(3)_____

For older students who are keeping a Thinking Log, make a grid. Each day thereafter, students can write in the name of the shared book and check off its corresponding attributes on their personal grids. Consider having students complete comparative thinking statements similar to the following:

I think the most critical attribute of this book was
_____.

Today, of the two books I read, I preferred _____
because

(1)_____

(2)_____

(3)_____

Follow-up After each discussion of a book, use the large grid on the bulletin board to list all the attributes identified. **Suggestion:** Begin with the elements of a book. Add to the list fiction and nonfiction attributes. The first are easily identified and the new skill of using a grid will not be confused with delineating content attributes. Have students work through each book. Use the grid as a wrap-up of discussion or, if necessary, as a guideline to generate comments.

Transfer Lesson:
Natural Sciences/ Rock Awareness

Focus Activity Give each student a piece of bubble gum and have them identify the attributes of bubble gum as they chew away.

Objective To have students define attributes of their own rocks and to have them establish varied subgroups by discovering similar or different characteristics in a group of collected rocks.

Activity

Note: Young students are often expected to do an introductory unit on rocks. However, before they begin to understand the three major classifications of rocks, they should have an opportunity to observe rocks, touch rocks and describe rocks. (Note the three classifications and their simple rules listed in the side box.) In the future, when students are expected to learn about rocks, those students who have had opportunities to identify attributes in a nonthreatening situation will have the advantage—so will the teacher.

1. Each student, and you, need to bring a "special" rock to school. Older students can work in pairs to collect an egg-cartoon full of rocks on a class excursion. This will provide an assortment for later groupings.

2. Sit in a circle with the students. Tell them: "Each of you will get a chance to show your rock and to identify a couple of its attributes that can be seen or felt." Demonstrate, "My rock is black and is shaped like a dime."

3. Go around the circle eliciting descriptive attributes from each student.

4. If time permits, put all the rocks in the center. Mix them up and have the students, in turn, retrieve their rocks.

5. Continue the activity by putting the rocks in the center. Ask for a volunteer to return as many rocks to their owners as possible. You can help in this thinking and remembering process by asking, "Who had that rock shaped like a dime?" Or, "Can you remember who told us that her rock was red with sparkles?"

7. Next, ask for a volunteer to make a subgroup of rocks. Allow thinking time and be sure the attribute is verbally identified and visually identified when creating the new group.

Rock Classifications

- Igneous rocks are classified by the minerals in them, by the size of their crystals and by their dark or light color.

- Sedimentary rocks are stratified layers of different kinds of gravel, sand and clay.

- Metamorphic rocks were once either igneous or sedimentary rocks changed by heat, pressure or chemicals.

Source: *The Beginners' Story of Minerals and Rocks,* by Melvin Keene

8. Draw large circles on a bulletin board. Label the circles with the rock classifications defined. Put the name of each rock owner in the appropriate circle or circles. Mix up the rocks, regroup them and list the names again. Once more, mix up the rocks, regroup them and list the names appropriately. Note, some rocks will have been in more than one group.

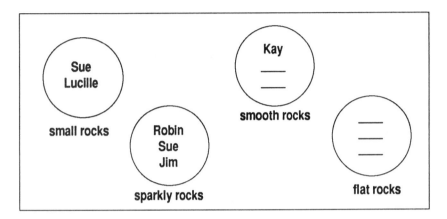

9. The preceding activity is an excellent preparation for Venn diagrams. If your class is developmentally ready, do a Venn diagram.

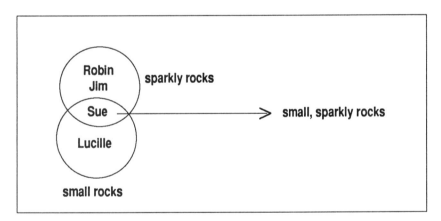

Metacognitive Processing
With their own rocks in hand, have students dictate for a language experience chart a list of ways that their rocks were grouped. Use the opportunity to introduce or practice positive and negative grouping. For example:

Smooth	Not smooth
Dark	Not dark
Black	Not black
Big	Not big

A two-column chart is an excellent visual tool. Have students complete the following sentence out loud or in their Thinking Logs:

> If I had a set of rocks to put into subsets, I would have to . . . . (Or, "If I had a set of rocks, I'd make Rocky Road Ice Cream!")

Follow-up Save the rocks for a few days, allowing time for repeated group activities. Provide library books with detailed pictures of rocks for interested students. Have a small group of students sort the rocks according to size or shade (dark to light). Afterward, students may want to make a face on their rocks with markers or pens.

Evaluation of Skills:

1. Have students identify, orally or in writing, the critical attributes of

   fiction and nonfiction books
   or
   various shapes studied
   or
   a group of rocks

2. Have students complete the following sentences out loud or in their Thinking Logs:

   Attributes are important because . . . .

   Attributes are like _____
   because both_____.

Thinking For
Problem Solving
Level I

Finding Problems and Solutions

Thinking Skill:

Finding Problems and Solutions

To live is to have problems, and to solve problems is to grow intellec-tually.

—*J.P. Gilford*

Model Lesson:

Lesson Objective To identify three steps of creative problem-solving.

Key Vocabulary Fact finding, idea finding, solution find-ing and brainstorming.

Looking Back Students have had opportunities to think creatively. They have brainstormed with fluency and flexibility, but *without* judgment or comment. In addition, they have practiced critical thinking in their analysis of classified items.

Getting Ready Students begin problem solving as infants. For example, a brightly colored, distant object attracts a child, and his or her body begins to move, squirm, crawl and walk to reach the object. If this object becomes a "brick wall" in the child's path, the child investigates how to get through, over, around or under it. A brick wall need not be a *physical* barrier; daily frustrations and emotions can also be brick walls. Take time to reflect on the creative problem-solving young students do during their play time and during their uncountable flashes of curiosity.

We must capitalize on this natural problem-solving skill in all students by verbalizing, identifying, sharing solutions and promoting reasoned judgments. We cannot expect logical decision making from young adults if we don't teach them early in their schooling how to recognize a problem and how to work with it.

In *Applied Imagination,* Alex F. Osborn offers an effective model for problem solving. We can teach this model with young students. Use a transparency, handout or poster to display Osborn's three-step model.

Osborn's 3 Steps to Problem Solving

1. Fact Finding
2. Idea Finding
3. Solution Finding

Steps 2 and 3 depend on the spontaneity and fluency of student input. Be aware of overload on Step 1.

Note: When students have an understanding of Osborn's three-step process, introduce Sidney J. Parnes' six-step model. (As with learning sentence structures, students need to master simple sentences or problems before they can understand compound and complex sentences or problems.) Parnes' three additional steps include sensing a problem, selecting and stating a problem, and acceptance finding, which answers "How are we going to do what we have determined should be done?"

When your students begin to practice the strategies of creative problem-solving, they will recognize problems quickly and will work toward solutions with less frustration and more understanding.

The new strategies must be applied over and over again. Research suggests that skills need to be done 10 to 15 times before you can expect transfer. Classrooms afford numerous opportunities in curriculum areas, classroom management and personal development to practice problem solving.

Begin a model for creative problem-solving early . . . reap the benefits forever!

At-A-Glance Initiate the idea of problem solving by identifying a specific problem. Brainstorm solutions, striving for fluency and creativity. Next, review each of the solutions to determine which are practical/impractical, possible/impossible and useful or nonuseful. This is not a "perfect solution" activity. Many acceptable solutions will be identified and applied as the situation warrants. Through practice, students will become aware of the three-step process. Follow up with transfer lessons across curriculum areas and in situational problems.

Focus Activity Set up a barrier in the classroom and have the students figure out ways to get around it.

Activity Objective To have students find the primary problem (identification and clarification by you may be necessary), brainstorm ideas and evaluate solutions to a problem that you have presented in a general statement.

Activity

1. Choosing a time period that allows you flexibility and ample time to complete the lesson, review the idea collecting (brainstorming) guidelines in the Brain Game:
   - Record ideas exactly as stated.
   - Record duplicates if offered.
   - Withhold all comments.
   - Remind (by example, not by a statement) students to piggyback on other ideas.
   - Eliminate the time limit if students are experienced enough in idea collecting.
   - Review the list orally and visually.
   - Guess how many ideas were collected.
   - Count the actual number of ideas.
   - Compare the guesses with the actual count.

2. Choose an interesting, age-appropriate problem. It should be relative either to your curriculum involvement at the time or a current classroom activity or event. Do not "muddy the waters" with too many sub-problems. At first, keep the main problem simple and definitive. Clarify the problem when necessary.

3. Present the problem in a general statement orally and visually:
   a. Say it.

Materials Needed

- ☐ Idea Collecting guidelines on transparency, handouts or poster

- ☐ Problem activity appropriate to class or transparency or handout of sample problem

- ☐ Lined chart paper

- ☐ Chart stand or masking tape

- ☐ Marking pencils

- ☐ Strips of paper

- ☐ Thinking Log

    b. Write it on chart paper.

    c. Give each student a copy of the problem written exactly as you presented it.

4. Following Osborn's three steps to problem solving, have the students find facts, ideas and solutions to the problem you presented.

SAMPLE PROBLEM-SOLVING ACTIVITY

> It is 1:30 p.m., 30 minutes until gym class with Mr. Smith, the students' favorite teacher. The principal sends a message: "The gym is being painted. All gym classes are cancelled."

Step 1: Fact Finding

- Ask, "What is the problem?" Wait three to ten seconds for a response and three to ten seconds after the response.

- The primary problem—What are the students going to do at 2:00 p.m.?—needs to be identified. Once someone verbalizes this as the problem, affirm it as the real problem and move to the next step. If, however, the suggested problems do not target the primary one, follow up with questions such as: "Yes, the paint will be wet, but it will still be wet at 3:00 p.m. Will that be a problem for us then? Why not?" You need to either draw out the primary problem or identify it and move on to Step 2.

Step 2: Idea Finding

> We cannot go to the gym today. What will we do at 2:00 p.m.?

- Say: "We cannot go to the gym today. That's a problem. We need to brainstorm ideas for what we can do at 2:00 p.m."

- Determine what time limits, if any, are suitable to this problem-solving activity and the age and experience of your students. Record the ideas following the idea collecting guidelines in the Brain Game. You may want to give an example. For instance, "We can play checkers at 2:00 p.m."

Step 3: Solution Finding

- After collecting ideas, tell students that some of the ideas can be done at 2:00 p.m. and some cannot. Go through all of the ideas

THINKING FOR PROBLEM SOLVING

one idea at a time, beginning with your suggestion to play checkers, and ask "Is this possible or impossible in the class-room?" If the idea is possible, leave it on the list and move to the next idea. If the idea is impossible to do in the classroom, cross it off the list.

- Tell the students that all of the ideas remaining on the chart paper are possible and that at 2:00 p.m. they will get to choose which one they want to do. Ask, "How many choices will each of you have?"

- Offer the students their choice of free time at 2:00 p.m.

Metacognitive Processing After the free time, tell the class: "We had a problem today and you solved it! How did you solve it? Why did you have so many activities to choose from during gym time?"

OPTIONAL PROCESSING

For younger students: Have them fold a piece of paper in half and ask them to draw both the gym being painted and the activity they chose to do. If time permits, let each student dictate a sentence about the activity to take home with the picture that day. This type of hand-made, student activity is an excellent parent "communicator" as opposed to a standard ditto.

For older students: Have them write and complete the following sentences in their Thinking Logs:

When we collected ideas today, I discovered . . .

I was pleased with our problem-solving results today because . . .

Short Practices:

FOR YOUNGER STUDENTS
- Read, recite or learn with the class the nursery rhyme "Humpty Dumpty." Identify the primary problem. Collect ideas for putting Humpty Dumpty together and evaluate which ones would work and which would be more difficult to accomplish.

FOR OLDER STUDENTS

■ Present a situation that relates to responsibilities children have at home or at school. For example tell the students: "You just accepted your first dogsitting job. Your neighbors took a weekend trip to their cottage and they left their dog in their garage. You agreed to feed, water and walk the dog early each morning and each evening. While you were at school, they left. Now it is 6:00 Friday evening. As you leave your house to take care of the dog, you realize the key for your neighbor's garage is in your desk at school." Ask, "What is your biggest problem?"

Students need to identify the primary problem. Through discussion, identify the primary problem and record it on the chalkboard:

> You need to feed, water and walk the dog. How do you get to the dog to take care of it?

Collect ideas in a large group setting or in small, random groupings. Remind the students that in mapping, as in idea collecting, all ideas are acceptable. Using the identified problem as the starting point, map the collected ideas in a simple web pattern on the board or a transparency. **Note:** Some students will have opinions and justifications about where their ideas "must" be placed on the map. Tell them that A MAP DISPLAYS A CREATIVE THINKING PROCESS—ONE'S MAPPING CANNOT BE WRONG, but it might be different. If the skill of mapping has been previously taught, you may want to increase the level of sophistication and involvement in the web. (See the sample idea map on page 36.)

When you have finished making the map, review each branch and discuss the ideas. The purpose of collecting ideas is to teach students to ACCEPT MULTIPLE IDEAS AND MULTIPLE SOLUTIONS—YOU NEED NOT ARRIVE AT THE "BEST" SOLUTION.

As a follow-up, have each student choose a solution and either draw, role play or write (in dictation, sentences, paragraphs, short stories etc.) about that choice. Solving problems can be a stimuli for writing experiences. Consider using the Thinking Log to have students map a similar problem—for example, "You lost your library book!"

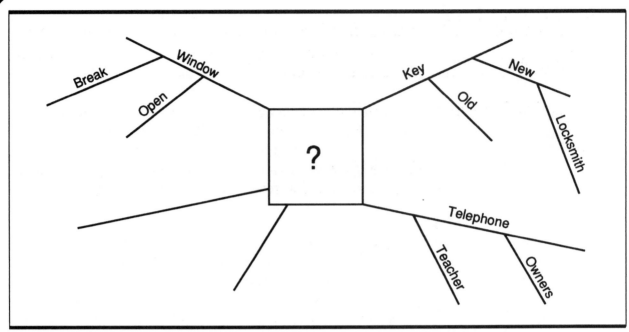

Idea Map

FOR ALL STUDENTS

■ Rarely does a day go by that teachers do not have to deal with one or more of the following student situations:

"I don't have a pencil."
"I don't have a red crayon."
"I am out of paper."
"Someone keeps taking my seat on the bus."

Be alert to these and other problems you have solved routinely in the past. Students need many opportunities to practice solving problems. Use these situations to let the students practice the techniques of problem solving: identifying the problem, collecting ideas for solving the problem, reviewing the solutions for the best one or ones.

Take time to work through the three problem-solving steps early in the year. Post the lists of ideas generated for various problems and let the students continue to add new ideas to them. If young students help identify the problem, help collect ideas for solving the problem and help analyze ideas for the best solution or solutions, then they will more readily understand advanced problem solving and decision making in the future. With carefully planned groundwork, classroom disruptions such as, "I can't find ..." and "I don't have ..." should be minimized.

Transfer Lesson: Literature

Focus Activity Introduce the book *Caps For Sale* by Esphyr Slobodkina. Read the first 10 pages to the students—up to the part where the text reads:

"The peddler looked at the monkeys. The monkeys looked at the peddler. He didn't know what to do. Finally he spoke to them."

Objective To introduce a problem situation as presented in children's literature and to practice collecting creative and multiple ideas.

Activity

1. Tell the students, "Today, using Osborn's three problem-solving steps, we are going to identify the peddler's problem, collect ideas for possible solutions and review those ideas."

STEP 1: FACT FINDING

2. Ask, "What is the peddler's problem?" Students may identify numerous problems. For example:

The monkeys have the hats.
The monkeys won't give back the hats.
He can't reach the hats.

These are all problems, but the primary problem is that he needs his hats to sell because that's his job. With young students this can become very confusing so don't spend too much time discussing. Identify the problem and move on.

3. Write the primary problem on the chart paper or chalkboard:

> The peddler needs to sell his hats. How can he get them from the monkeys?

STEP 2: IDEA FINDING

4. Review the idea collecting rules for:
Fluency (accepting multiple, creative ideas)
Flexibility (piggybacking)
Being Nonjudgmental (making no comments)

5. Collect ideas to solve the peddler's problem and write them on a list.

STEP 3: SOLUTION FINDING

6. Review each idea on the list. Consider the following activities to help review:

    ■ Ask for volunteers to role play the monkeys. As you move down the list of collected ideas, have students role play the peddler's actions for some of the solutions. IMPORTANT: Follow up with a discussion on possible/impossible and useful/nonuseful ideas or solutions.

    ■ Use "wraparound" and "forced response" techniques to involve all students in discussing the ideas. (See the side box for these strategies.) Begin with the first solution on your list of collected ideas. Determine how you will wrap around—through the entire room, down one row of students, around one grouping etc.—and work through the list reading one idea at a time. Follow each idea with a student stating: "That's a good idea because. . . ." If students have had enough experience, work through the list again having them say, "That might not work because. . . ."

Discussion Techniques

■ The **wraparound** requires each student, in turn, to respond to a question/problem with an answer or with the statement, "I pass."

■ With **forced response**, a statement is made or read by one person and another person responds by saying something similar to, "That's a good idea because..." or "I like that idea because. . . ."

Metacognitive Processing Tell the students: "The peddler in this book had a problem. Several ways to solve the problem were suggested. One finally worked!" On the chart paper, transparency or chalkboard write (or hand out this prompter):

> When we have a problem, we should . . .

Have younger students dictate what they might do when faced with a problem.

Have older students complete the following sentences in their Thinking Logs:

> When I have a problem to solve, I need to . . .

> When we did the wraparound activity, I was able to . . .

Follow-up Ask students what problems they have seen people face on TV, in a book, at home or at school. Ask the students to discuss or write in their logs how that problem was handled. Would they have handled it differently or the same? Why or why not?

Transfer Lesson:
Art/ Situational Problems

Focus Activity Have two students role play fighting over a chair. Collect ideas about the problem and possible solutions.

Objective To identify problems, collect solutions and make choices that will result in a creative product.

Activity

1. At the beginning of an art period, tell students they are going to make a special picture today. Don't give any other details, just let them think about what you said.

2. Practice wait time. Be patient. Someone will ask, "What kind?" or, "How are we going to do it?" Say, "That's one of our problems today because I'm not going to tell you what to do or how to do it. However, I will show you a way to solve this problem of what do I do?"

3. Use a prepared, four-column chart on a transparency or poster.

Art Picture

What Will I Draw?	What Size Picture?	What Will I Use?	What Color Paper?

Say, "Let's start with the first problem, what will I draw?" In the first column on the left, use the heading WHAT WILL I DRAW?

"Let's collect some ideas of what you might draw. We will have one minute (or whatever amount of time you find appropriate). Remember the rules: think of lots of ideas, piggyback off of others' ideas and make no comments. I will write your ideas in this column." Suggest one idea to the class, then set the timer and let the students suggest their own ideas.

4. When the time limit is up or when the students run out of ideas, say: "Now we have many ideas, but we still have some problems. Can anyone help identify another problem?" If no suggestion is forthcoming, ask the students what size they want to make their project. Tell them there are many different sizes of pictures. Move to the second column and head it WHAT SIZE PICTURE? Collect sizes. You may find younger students using descriptive words such as tiny and big and older students being more specific about the size.

5. Ask, "What other problem do we have before we can begin our picture? Allow the students time to think. If no suggestion is forthcoming, define the next problem, "What are you going to use to make the picture?" Move to column three and title it WHAT WILL I USE? and have students brainstorm things they can use to draw the picture.

6. "We have many ideas, sizes and ways to draw our pictures, but we have one more problem. . . . If no one identifies the type of paper or the color of the paper, move to column four and title it WHAT COLOR PAPER? Note, the order of the columns depends on the flow of the students' thinking and ideas.

7. Review each list with the class.

8. Depending on the age level of your students, your time schedule, the available materials and your energy level for that day, you may use these lists in at least two ways. Ideally, each child should choose one item from each column to set guidelines for creating a personal picture. Alternatively though, you can control the activity more by pulling numbers out of a "hat"— third one down is the subject, the fifth one down is the size etc.—creating less confusion, but still allowing for individual creativity.

9. Enjoy! Encourage students to share why they chose the elements they did. As you move through the classroom, comment on one of their choices, either the subject matter, paper size, paper color or materials.

Metacognitive Processing

With younger students say: "You solved a big problem today—what and how to draw a picture—by finding the little problems. What did you do that gave you lots of ideas? What would you have to know if I asked you to make me a pair of shoes? How would you find out?"

Have older students use their Thinking Logs to complete the following sentences:

The best idea for a picture today was . . .
The craziest idea for a picture today was . . .
The most boring idea for a picture today was . . .

Follow-up Whichever method students use for choosing their project, work through it with them so they understand how the columns can help solve a problem. Let the students create various combinations so they see the "big picture."

Evaluation of Skills:

1. Capitalize on a student's problem, such as John forgot his lunch money, Mary did not return her library book, or the bees keep bothering us in our classroom. Present the situation and ask students to identify the problem that has to be solved.

   Once the problem is recorded, ask, "How do we find a solution for this problem?" Have students collect ideas for finding solutions.

2. Choose two solutions and have the students complete (orally for younger students and as a log entry for older students) the following sentence:

   That's a good idea because . . .

3. Choose two other solutions and have the students complete (orally or in writing) the following sentence:

   That might not be possible or practical because . . .

Keep Them Thinking
Level I

Masters Appendix

Premise 1

The teacher is the architect of the intellect.

A teacher affects eternity. He never knows where his influence ends.
-Henry Adams

Premise 2

The student is the capable apprentice.

'Come to the edge,' he said.
They said, 'We are afraid.'
'Come to the edge,' he said. They came.
He pushed them…and they flew.
-Appollinaire

Premise 3

Thinking is more basic than the basics— it frames all learning.

Intelligent behavior is knowing what to do when you don't know what to do.
-Arthur Costa

Idea Collecting (Brainstorming) Guidelines

- Record ideas exactly as stated, (including duplicates).

- Withhold all comments.

- Remind (by example, not by a statement) students to piggy-back on other ideas.

- Eliminate the time limit if students are experienced enough at idea collecting.

- Review the list visually and orally.

- Remove duplicates.

- Guess how many ideas were collected.

- Count the actual number of ideas.

- Recount them in another way.

- Compare the guesses with the actual count.

- Use the originals and duplicates again and again.

TODAY'S BRAIN GAME ROOM _____

Date _____

Today we collected _____
in class.

You may wish to spend a few minutes reviewing and extending the "idea collecting" (brainstorming) activity by letting or helping your child do one or more of the following:

- _____
- _____
- _____
- _____
- _____

Enjoy! Enjoy! Remember, 10 to 15 minutes is adequate and valuable! Thanks for your help.

Evaluation of Skills

1. Explain some ideas or rules about collecting ideas for a Language Experience Chart to be displayed in the room.

2. Draw pictures of a class idea collecting.

3. Record in your Thinking Logs:

   Three things I know about idea collecting are

   (1)_____

   (2)_____

   (3)_____

Attribute
Grid

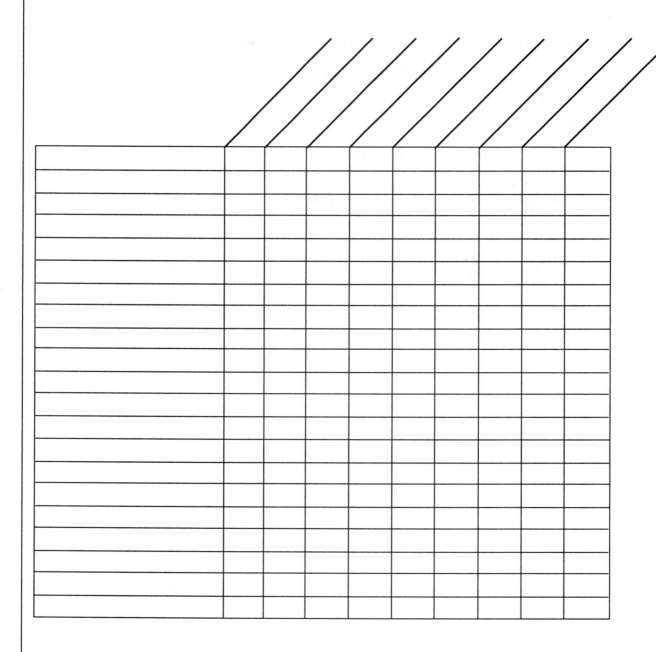

Rock Classifications

■ Igneous rocks are classified by the minerals in them, by the size of their crystals and by their dark or light color.

■ Sedimentary rocks are stratified layers of different kinds of gravel, sand and clay.

■ Metamorphic rocks were once either igneous or sedimentary rocks changed by heat, pressure or chemicals.

Source: *The Beginners' Story of Minerals and Rocks*, by Melvin Keene

Evaluation of Skills:

1. Identify, orally or in writing, the critical attributes of

   fiction and nonfiction books
   or
   various shapes studied
   or
   a group of rocks

2. Complete the following sentences out loud or in your Thinking Logs:

   Attributes are important because . . . .

   Attributes are like _____

   because
   both_____

Osborn's 3 Steps
to Problem Solving

1. Fact Finding

2. Idea Finding

3. Solution Finding

Sample Problem-Solving Activity

It is 1:30 p.m., 30 minutes until gym class with Mr. Smith, the students' favorite teacher. The principal sends a message: "The gym is being painted. All gym classes are cancelled."

Idea Map

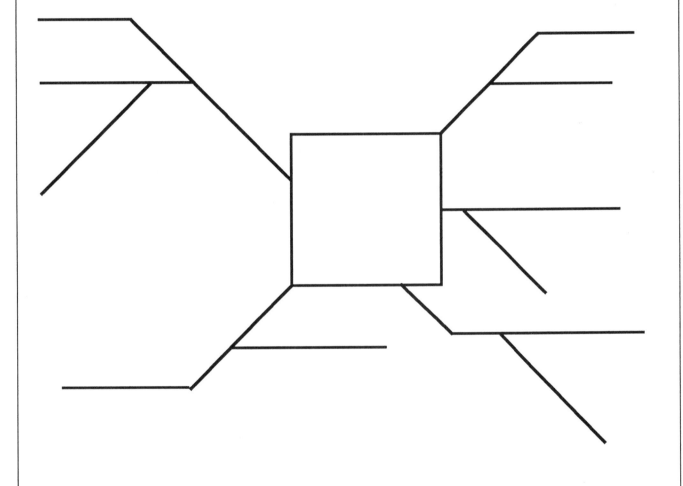

Evaluation
of Skills:

1. Identify the problem that has to be solved.

2. Complete the following sentence:

   That's a good idea because . . .

3. Complete the following sentence:

   That might not be possible or practical because . . .

Worksheet Model for Original Lessons

To assist you in creating your own thinking lessons that follow the model explained in the introduction, we have included a blank worksheet which outlines the major components. Feel free to photocopy these worksheet pages. Fill them in with your own lesson content to tailor thinking lessons specifically to your class' needs.

Lesson Objective

Key Vocabulary

Looking Back

Getting Ready

At-A-Glance

Materials Needed

Focus Activity

Activity Objective

Activity

Metacognitive Processing

Bibliography

Ainsworth-Land, V., & Fletcher, N. (1979). *Making waves with creative problem solving.* Buffalo, NY: D.O.K.

Anderson, L.W., & Jones, B.F. (1981). Designing instructional strategies which facilitate learning for mastery. *Educational Psychologist, 16,* 121–138.

Anderson, R. et al. (1985). *Becoming a nation of readers: The report of the Commission on Reading.* Pittsburgh: National Academy of Education.

Anderson, R., & Pearson, P.D. (1985). A schema-theoretic view of basic processes in reading comprehension. In P.D. Pearson (Ed.), *Handbook of reading research.* New York: Longman.

Anderson, T.H., & Armbruster, B.B. (1984). Content area textbooks. In R.C. Anderson, J. Osborn, & R.J. Tierney (Eds.), *Learning to read in American schools: Basal readers and content texts.* Hillsdale, NJ: Erlbaum.

Armbruster, B.B., Echols, L.H., & Brown, A.L. (1983). *The role of metacognition in reading to learn: A developmental perspective.* Urbana, IL: University of Illinois Center for the Study of Reading.

Bellanca, J. (1991). *Building a caring, cooperative classroom.* Palatine, IL: Skylight Publishing.

Bellanca, J. (1990). *The cooperative think tank.* Palatine, IL: Skylight Publishing.

Bellanca, J. (1990). *Keep them thinking, Level III.* Palatine, IL: Skylight Publishing.

Bellanca, J. (1984). *Quality circles for educators.* Palatine, IL: Skylight Publishing.

Bellanca, J., & Fogarty, R. (1990). *Blueprints for thinking in the cooperative classroom.* Palatine, IL: Skylight Publishing.

Bellanca, J., & Fogarty, R. (1986). *Catch them thinking.* Palatine, IL: Skylight Publishing.

Berliner, D.C. (1984). The half-full glass: A review of research in teaching. In P.L. Hosford (Ed.), *Using what we know about teaching.* Alexandria, VA: Association for Supervision and Curriculum Development.

Beyer, B.K. (1984, March). Improving thinking skills—defining the problem. *Phi Delta Kappan,* pp. 486-490.

Beyer, B.K. (1983, November). Common sense about teaching thinking skills. *Educational Leadership,* pp. 57-62.

Biondi, A. (Ed.). (1972). *The creative process.* Buffalo, NY: D.O.K.

Black, H., & Black, S. (1981). *Figural analogies.* Pacific Grove, CA: Midwest Publications.

Bloom, B.S. (1981). *All our children learning. A primer for parents, teachers, and educators.* New York: McGraw-Hill.

Bloom, B.S. (Ed.). (1956). *Taxonomy of educational objectives: Cognitive domain.* New York: David McKay.

Brown, A.L. (1980). Metacognitive development and reading. In R.J. Spiro, B.C. Bruce, & W. F. Brewer (Eds.), *Theoretical issues in reading comprehension.* Hillsdale, NJ: Erlbaum.

Burns, M. (1976). *The book of think or how to solve a problem twice your size.* Boston, MA: Little, Brown and Company.

Campbell, T.C., et al. (1980). A teacher's guide to the learning cycle. A Piagetian-based approach to college instruction. In R.G. Fuller, et al. (Eds.), *Piagetian programs in higher education* (pp. 27-46). Lincoln, NE: ADAPT, University of Nebraska-Lincoln.

Carnine, D., & Silbert, J. (1979). *Direct instruction reading.* Columbus, OH: Merrill Publishing.

Carpenter, E.T. (1980). Piagetian interview of college students. In R.G. Fuller, et al. (Eds.), *Piagetian programs in higher education* (pp. 15-21). Lincoln, NE: ADAPT, University of Nebraska-Lincoln.

Carpenter, T.P., Corbitt, M.K., Kepner, H., Linquist, M.M., & Reys, R.W. (1980, October). Students' affective responses to mathematics: National assessment results. *Educational Leadership,* pp. 24-37, 52, 531-539.

Chase, L. (1975). *The other side of the report card.* Glenview, IL: Scott Foresman.

Clark, B. (1979). *Growing up gifted.* Columbus, OH: Merrill Publishing.

Clement, J. (1982). Algebra word problem solutions: Thought processes underlying a common misconception. *Journal for Research in Mathematics Education, 13*, 16-30.

Clement, J. (1982). Students' preconceptions in introductory mechanics. *American Journal of Physics, 50*, 66-71.

College Entrance Examination Board. (1983). *Academic preparation for college: What students need to know and be able to do.* New York: College Board.

Convigtona, M.V., Crutchfield, R.S., Davies, L., & Olton, R.M. (1974). *The productive thinking program: A course in learning to think.* Columbus, OH: Merrill Publishing.

Costa, A. (1991). *The school as a home for the mind.* Palatine, IL: Skylight Publishing, Inc.

Costa, A. (Ed.). (1985). *Developing minds.* Alexandria, VA: Association for Supervision and Curriculum Development.

Costa, A. (1984). Mediating the metacognitive. *Educational Leadership, 42*(2), 57-62.

Costa, A. (1981, October). Teaching for intelligent behavior. *Educational Leadership*, pp. 29-32.

Costa, A., Bellanca, J., & Fogarty, R. (Eds.). (1992). *If minds matter: A foreword to the future, Vols. I & II*. Palatine, IL: Skylight Publishing.

Costa, A., & Lowery, L. (1989). *Techniques for teaching thinking*. Pacific Grove, CA: Midwest Publications.

Craik, F.I.M., & Lockhard, R.S. (1972). Levels of processing: Framework for memory research. *Journal of Verbal Learning and Verbal Behavior, II,* pp. 671-684.

Duchastel, P.C. (1982). Textual display techniques. In D. Jonnasen (Ed.), *Principles for structuring, designing, and displaying text*. Englewood Cliffs, NJ: Educational Technology Publications.

Durkin, D. (1978-1979). What classroom observations reveal about reading comprehension instruction. *Reading Research Quarterly, 15,* 481-533.

Easterling, J., & Pasanen, J. (1979). *Confront, construct, complete*. Rochell Park, NJ: Hayden.

Eberle, B. (1982). *SCAMPER: Games for imagination development*. Buffalo, NY: D.O.K.

Eberle, B. (1982). *Visual thinking*. Buffalo, NY: D.O.K.

Eberle, B., & Stanish, B. (1980). *CPS for kids*. Buffalo, NY: D.O.K.

Edwards, B. (1979). *Drawing on the right side of the brain*. Los Angeles: J.P. Tarcher.

Eggen, P.D., & Kauchak, D.P. (1979). *Strategies for teachers: Teaching content and thinking skills*. Englewood Cliffs, NJ: Prentice-Hall.

Elbow, P. (1973). *Writing without teachers*. New York: Oxford University Press.

Ennis, R.H., & Norris, S.P. (1989). *Evaluating critical thinking*. Pacific Grove, CA: Midwest Publications.

Ferguson, M. (1980). *The aquarian conspiracy*. Los Angeles: J.P. Tarcher.

Feuerstein, R., & Jensen, M.R. (1980). Instructional enrichment: Theoretical bias, goals, and instruments. *The Education Form,* pp. 401-423.

Fiestrizer, C.E. (1984). *The making of a teacher*. Washington, DC: National Center for Education Information.

50-state survey on critical thinking initiatives. (1985). Washington, DC: American Federation of Teachers.

Fiske, E. (1984, September 9). Concern over schools spurs extensive efforts at reform. *New York Times,* 1, 30.

Fogarty, R. (1991). *The mindful school: How to integrate the curricula.* Palatine, IL: Skylight Publishing.

Fogarty, R. (1990). *Keep them thinking: Level II.* Palatine, IL: Skylight Publishing.

Fogarty, R. (1990). *Designs for cooperative interactions.* Palatine, IL: Skylight Publishing.

Fogarty, R., & Bellanca, J. (1986). *Teach them thinking.* Palatine, IL: Skylight Publishing.

Fogarty, R., & Bellanca, J. (1985). *Patterns for thinking—Patterns for transfer.* Palatine, IL: Skylight Publishing.

Fogarty, R., & Opeka, K. (1988). *Start them thinking.* Palatine, IL: Skylight Publishing.

Fogarty, R., Perkins, D., & Barell, J. (1992). *The mindful school: How to teach for transfer.* Palatine, IL: Skylight Publishing.

Gallagher, J. (1985). *Teaching the gifted child.* Boston: Allyn & Bacon.

Gallelli, G. (1977). *Activity mindset guide.* Buffalo, NY: D.O.K.

Gifford, B.R. (1985, March 20). We must interrupt the cycle of minority-group failure. *Education Week, sec. IV,* 17-24.

Glatthorn, A. (1984). *Differentiated supervision.* Alexandria, VA: Association for Supervision and Curriculum Development.

Good, T.L. (1981, February). Teacher expectations and student perceptions. *Educational Leadership,* pp. 415-422.

Good, T.L., & Brophy, J. E. (1984). *Looking in classrooms.* Cambridge, MA: Harper and Row.

Guilford, J.P. (1975). *Way beyond the I.Q.* Buffalo, NY: Creative Education Foundation.

Hansen, J., & Pearson, P.D. (1983). An instructional study: Improving the inferential comprehension of good and poor fourth-grade readers. *Journal of Educational Psychology, 75,* 821-829.

Harnadek, A. (1980). *Critical thinking.* Pacific Grove, CA: Midwest Publications.

Harnadek, A. (1977). *Basic thinking skills: Analogies-D.* Pacific Grove, CA: Midwest Publications.

Harnadek, A. (1977). *Basic thinking skills: Patterns.* Pacific Grove, CA: Midwest Publications.

Herber, H.L. (1978). *Reading in the content areas: Text for teachers.* Englewood Cliffs, NJ: Prentice-Hall.

Hodgkinson, H.L. (1985). *All one system: Demography of schools, kindergarten through graduate school.* Washington, DC: Institute for Educational Leadership.

Jenkins, J. (1974). Remember the old theory of memory? Well, forget it! *American Psychologist, 29,* 785-795.

Johnson, R., & Johnson, D. (1987). *Learning together and alone: Cooperative, competitive, and individualistic learning.* New York: Prentice-Hall.

Johnson, R., & Johnson, D. (1986). *Circles of learning: Cooperation in the classroom.* Alexandria, VA: Association for Supervision and Curriculum Development.

Jones, B.F., Amiran, M.R., & Katims, M. (1985). Teaching cognitive strategies and text structures within language arts programs. In S.F. Chipman & R. Glaser (Eds.), *Thinking and learning skills: Relating basic research to instructional practices, 1.* Hillsdale, NJ: Erlbaum.

Jones, B.F., & Spady, W.G. (1985). Enhanced mastery learning and quality of instruction. In D.V. Levine (Ed.), *Improving student achievement through mastery learning programs.* San Francisco, CA: Jossey-Bass.

Karplus, R. (1974). *Science curriculum improvement study, teacher's handbook.* Berkeley, CA: University of California, Berkeley.

Larkin, J. (1983). Research on science education. In A.M. Lesgold & F. Reif (Eds.), *Education: Realizing the potential.* Washington, DC: Office of the Assisted Secretary for Educational Research and Improvement.

Larkin, J., McDermott, J., Simon, D.P., & Simon, H.A. (1980, June 20). Expert and novice performance in solving physics problems. *Science*, pp. 1335-1342.

Lazear, D. (1991). *Seven ways of knowing.* Palatine, IL: Skylight Publishing.

Lazear, D. (1991). *Seven ways of teaching.* Palatine, IL: Skylight Publishing.

Maraviglia, C. (1978). *Creative problem-solving think book.* Buffalo, NY: D.O.K.

Marcus, S., & McDonald, P. (1990). *Tools for the cooperative classroom.* Palatine, IL: Skylight Publishing.

Maria, K., & McGinitie, W.H. (1982). Reading comprehension disabilities, knowledge structures, and non-accommodating text-processing strategies. *Annals of Dyslexia, 32,* 33-59.

Markle, S.M. (1975). They teach concepts, don't they? *Educational Researcher, 4,* 3-9.

Mayer, R.E. (1984). Aids to text comprehension. *Educational Psychologist, 19,* 30-42.

McCloskey, M., Carmazza, A., & Green, B. (1980, December 5). Curvilinear motion in the absence of external forces: Naive beliefs about the motion of objects. *Science,* pp. 1139-1141.

National Commission on Excellence in Education. (1983). *A nation at risk: The imperative for educational reform.* Washington, DC: U.S. Department of Education.

National Consortium for Educational Excellence. (1984). *An agenda for educational renewal: A report to the secretary of education, United States Department of Education.* Nashville, TN: Vanderbilt University, Peabody College.

National Institute of Education. (1980). *Who's keeping score?* Washington, DC: McLeod Corporation.

Nickerson, R.S. (1983). Computer programming as a vehicle for teaching thinking skills. *Journal of Philosophy for Children, 4,* 3-4.

Nickerson, R.S. (1982). *Understanding understanding* (BBN Report No. 5087).

Nickerson, R.S., et al. (1984). *The teaching of learning strategies* (BBN Report No. 5578)

Nickerson, R.S., Perkins, D.N., & Smith, E. E. (1984). *Teaching thinking* (BBN Report No. 5575).

Nisbett, R., & Ross, L. (1980). *Human inference: Strategies and shortcomings of social judgment.* Englewood Cliffs, NJ: Prentice-Hall.

Noller, R. (1977). *Scratching the surface of creative problem-solving: A bird's-eye view of CPS.* Buffalo, NY: D.O.K.

Noller, R., Parnes, S., & Biondi, A. (1976). *Creative action book.* New York: Charles Scribner and Sons.

Noller, R., Treffinger, D., & Houseman, E. (1979). *It's a gas to be gifted* or *CPS for the gifted and talented.* Buffalo, NY: D.O.K.

Osborn, A.F. (1963). *Applied imagination.* New York: Charles Scribner and Sons.

Palincsar, A.S., & Brown, A.L. (1985). Reciprocal activities to promote reading with your mind. In T.L. Harris & E. Cooper (Eds.), *Reading, thinking, and concept development: Strategies for the classroom.* New York: The College Board.

Parnes, S. (1975). *Aha! Insights into creative behavior.* Buffalo, NY: D.O.K.

Parnes, S. (1972). *Creativity: Unlocking human potential.* Buffalo, NY: D.O.K.

Pearson, P.D., & Leys, M. (1985). Teaching comprehension. In T.L. Harris & E. Cooper (Eds.), *Reading, thinking, and concept development: Strategies for the classroom.* New York: The College Board.

Perkins, D., & Swartz, R. (1989). *Teaching thinking: Issues and approaches.* Pacific Grove, CA: Midwest Publications.

Peters, T. & Austin, N. (1985). *Passion for excellence.* New York: Random House.

Peters, T. & Waterman, R., Jr. (1982). *In search of excellence.* New York: Warner Communication.

Polette, N. (1981). *Exploring books for gifted programs.* Metuchen, NJ: Scarecrow Press.

Raths, L. (1967). *Teaching for thinking.* Columbus, OH: Merrill Publishing.

Resnick, L.B. (1984). Cognitive science as educational research: Why we need it now. In Learning Research and Development Center, *Improving education: Perspectives on educational research*. Pittsburgh, PA: University of Pittsburgh.

Rico, G.L. (1983). *Writing the natural way*. Los Angeles: J.P. Tarcher.

Rohwer, W.D. Jr. (1971). Prime time for education: Early childhood or adolescence? *Harvard Educational Review, 41,* 316-341.

Rosenshine, B. (1983). Teaching functions in instructional programs. *Elementary School Journal, 83,* 335-351.

Rosenshine, B., Harnischfeger, A., & Wallberg, H. (1985, March). *Classroom programs for school improvement*. Elmhurst, IL: North Central Regional Educational Laboratory.

Rowe, M.B. (1969). Science, silence and sanctions. *Science & Children, 6,* 11-13.

Rumelhart, D.E. (1980). Schemata: The building blocks of cognition. In R.J. Spiro, B.C. Bruce, & W.F. Brewer (Eds.), *Theoretical issues in reading comprehension*. Hillsdale, NJ: Erlbaum.

Scardamalia, M., Bereiter, C., & Fillion B. (1979). *The little red writing book: A source book of consequential writing activities*. Ontario, Canada: Pedagogy of Writing Project, O.I.S.E.

Schallert, D.L. (1980). The role of illustrations in reading comprehension. In R.J. Spiro, B.C. Bruce & W. F. Brewer (Eds.), *Theoretical issues in reading comprehension*. Hillsdale, NJ: Erlbaum.

Schoenfeld, A.H. (1980). Teaching problem-solving skills. *American Mathematical Monthly, 87*(10), 794-805.

Shuell, T.J. (1984, October). *The concept of learning in modern-day cognitive psychology*. Paper presented at the annual meeting of the Northeastern Educational Research Association, Ellenville, New York.

Shulman, L.S. (1984). Understanding pedagogy: Research for the improvement of teaching and teacher education. In Learning Research and Development Center, *Improving education: Perspectives on educational research*. Pittsburgh, PA: University of Pittsburgh.

Sirkin, J.R. (1985, May 8). All-black education agenda advocated: Press for excellence seen at odds with equity goal. *Education Week, sec. IV,* 1, 27.

Snyder, D.P. (1985). *The strategic context of education in America* (Future-Research Tech. Rep.). Washington, DC: National Education Association, Professional and Organization Development/Office of Planning.

The Southern Regional Education Board. (1985). *Teacher preparation: The anatomy of a college degree*. Atlanta: Author.

Spiro, R. (1980). Constructive processes in prose comprehension and recall. In R.J. Spiro, B.C. Bruce, & W.F. Brewer (Eds.), *Theoretical issues in reading comprehension.* Hillsdale, NJ: Erlbaum.

Sternberg, R.J. (1981, October). Intelligence as thinking and learning skills. *Educational Leadership,* pp. 18-21.

Task Force on Education for Economic Growth. (1983). *Action for excellence: A comprehensive plan to improve our nation's schools.* Washington, DC: Education Commission of the United States.

Tolkien, J.R.R. (1937). *The hobbit.* New York: Ballantine Books.

Torrance, E.P. (1979). *The search for satori and creativity.* Buffalo, NY: Creative Education Foundation and Great Neck, NY: Creative Synergetics Associates.

Trowbridge, D.E., & McDermott, L.C. (1980). Investigation of student understanding of the concept of velocity in one dimension. *American Journal of Physics, 48*(12), 1010-1028.

Tversky, A., & Kahneman, D. (1974, September 27). Judgment under uncertainty: Heuristics and biases. *Science,* pp. 1124-1131.

Underwood, V.L. (1982). *Self-management skills for college students: A program in how to learn.* Unpublished doctoral dissertation, University of Texas.

U.S. Department of Education. (1984). *The nation responds*: *Recent efforts to improve education.* Washington, DC: Author.

von Oech, R. (1983). *A whack on the side of the head.* New York: Warner Books.

Additional resources to increase your teaching expertise...

There are

one-story intellects,

two-story intellects, and three-story

intellects with skylights. All fact collectors who have

no aim beyond their facts are one-story men. Two-story men compare,

reason, generalize, using the labor of fact collectors as their own.

Three-story men idealize, imagine, predict—

their best illumination comes

from above the skylight.

—*Oliver Wendell*

Holmes

SKYLIGHT
PUBLISHING, INC.